ISBN: 978 – 9966 – 120 – 50 – 2

Front and back cover design: Maham Mushtak

To Pam,

Best wishes,

Mehreen

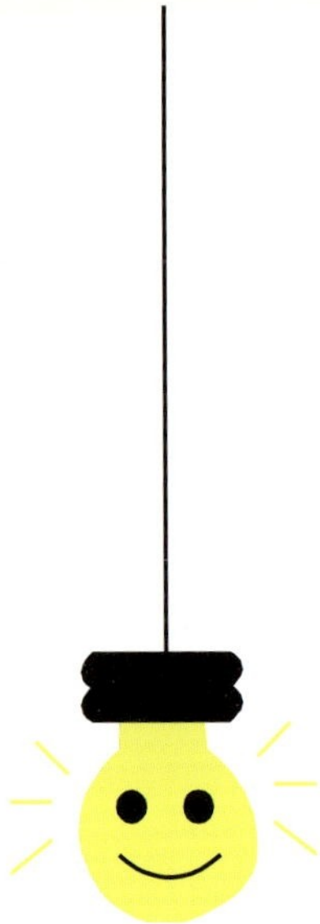

In the loving memory of my dad,

I love you and miss you ❤

Acknowledgements:

First and foremost, I would like to thank the Almighty for the strength and will power to accomplish this dream.

My heartfelt thank you to my parents for the constant support, motivation, and most of all, making this possible.

In making this book a success, there has been support from amazing people who have contributed towards enriching the content in one way or another.

I would like to thank Mehboob Lakha, my uncle, who has supported and guided me from the initiation of this book. Also, thanking my sister for the amazing book cover, thank you Maham.

I would also like to thank:

- Zainab Karim, author of Asiyah: A Quest for Self-love.
- Sakina NurMohamed

📖 Arifa Suleman, author of The Regeneration (theregenerationsite.wordpress.com)

"Happiness", along with the effort to understand, pursue, and achieve it is one of the biggest challenges of our era. It is in moments overwhelmed with any form of helplessness where quiet reflections hold the most meaning and have the greatest effect. Mehreen's poetry dives deep into these moments, pulling up all the sadness and converting it into something beautiful and worthy of happiness. Nothing is more therapeutic than the soothing words of poetry to calm a heart in distress, and by optimizing on that, Mehreen has created a wonderful little world in her book where we can break through the surface of our daily routine and breathe again."

Zainab Karim, author of Asiyah: A Quest for Self-love.

"Different people have different definitions of happiness. They prioritize certain factors over others so they find the maximum happiness at contentment in themselves. For example my formula to leading a happy life is being grateful for what I have and not comparing my story to anyone else. Also taking control of my mindset before it controls me. The main reason why I'd read this book is to learn more about someone else's perception. Learning about someone else's journey is truly eye opening. Would strongly recommend it to those that may be going through a tough phase where being happy isn't as easy."

Arifa Suleman, author of The Regeneration (theregenerationsite.wordpress.com)

That amazing moment when you get an answer to a question...

Preface:

Spectrum of happiness:

This book is dedicated to bring out positivity and happiness in people. In the challenging world today, it has become even more important to lead life happily and learn from situations that arise in life. All may not be in favor but they do take you through a worthwhile journey that may lead to an even better outcome than imagined. ***Spectrum of happiness*** aims to show that one can find happiness in different ways in life because every person has their own definition of being happy.

A life lived happily and memories made throughout make it worthwhile and pleasant to look back at milestones and achievements, and non-is too big or too small to celebrate.

Authors note:

This book began with a story, my story. I had a dream of writing a book, but I never took it up as a profession. This book is here to show you that no matter how big or small your dreams are; with hard work and good work ethic, they will all come true.

Every page depicts emotions that I have been through or something that I have observed in the course of writing this book.
All of us face challenges in life, and I did too.
Getting this book to you was a journey that has taken a few years and this time has been worth it.

The only advice I would give readers is to keep persistence in any task you begin and give it your 100%, you will welcome achievements that you never imagined you could.

Rules of reading this book:

Books don't usually have rules, however, this book is an initiation to spark active reading in today's reader, to help ponder and think. Reading in between the lines isn't just a famous phrase rather something we should do to nurture creativity and critical thinking.

This book consists of poems and spoken word pieces that are divided into sections.

1. Read each page with a calm mind and take the time to relate it to your own life by answering one simple question.
   "How did this make me happy?"

And don't give up! Keep looking until you get an answer because everyone has an answer for happiness described in every page of this book.

2. Make this habit that will help you see the immense bounties you have and be grateful rather than complain. This is one way to find happiness.

Journey towards the Golden Heart:

"The most truly generous persons are those who give silently without hope of praise or reward."

~ *Carol Ryrie Brink*

Generosity is usually considered as an act of giving away of tangible goods to help others. However, have we ever thought about the impact of our actions?

We may do something that means the world to a person - even bringing a smile on their face.
And through years passing by, we may forget that, but the person will always remember.

Always do well without the intention of getting back. You may not get back a tangible thing, but what you do get is a strange feeling in your heart - that of satisfaction and happiness.

Only the strongest people can sacrifice without making it evident.

Be the one
that lights up
not only their own
life, but the lives of
millions of people
around them

I WISH...

I wish I could make a difference,
I wish I could bring a change,
A revolution, a transformation...

Yes, I can! We can together!
We all have our part to play, and each
one of us can make a difference.

Don't wait for someone to begin,
initiate the start, and see the flow.
All this will seem like a dream, a good
dream.

Let us come out of our comfort zone
and support justice.
This is the least that we can do!

"There is no exercise better for the heart than reaching down and lifting people up."
~ John Holmes

The higher you go, don't look down but look upon those who are below you.

Although struggles teach you, but some moments hurt, and some may take long to forget if you hold on to your past.

Help them always by guiding, inspiring, and motivating them. See that you always spread happiness and light paving the way up for others.

Spending a little time goes a long way, although you may forget your good deed, others will always remember. What is better than being in someone's thoughts and prayers?

IS IT ALL ABOUT I, ME, AND MYSELF?

Sometimes I wonder why I should think about people at all times? Why is it so important?

I get an answer everyday! From sharing a chocolate, or spending time with a friend, or buying a gift.
It gives a different kind of happiness and excitement from within.

That is extreme happiness is true happiness.

The greatest happiness is not in always being perfect, rather helping someone who is not.

It is not guaranteed that whom you help will become perfect, but it builds a bond of friendship, companionship, a forever-lasting bond.

Don't refrain from helping,
Sharing knowledge will not decrease what you know; rather, it will grow even more.

In the race of excellence, don't forget your loved ones, humanity, and goodness.
The winner is not the one who reaches the finish line first, but the one who brings along everyone together.

Rather than winning, relationships are the most important, if you lose them on the way, then even a won race becomes bigger than a loss.

To the chosen ones - friendship

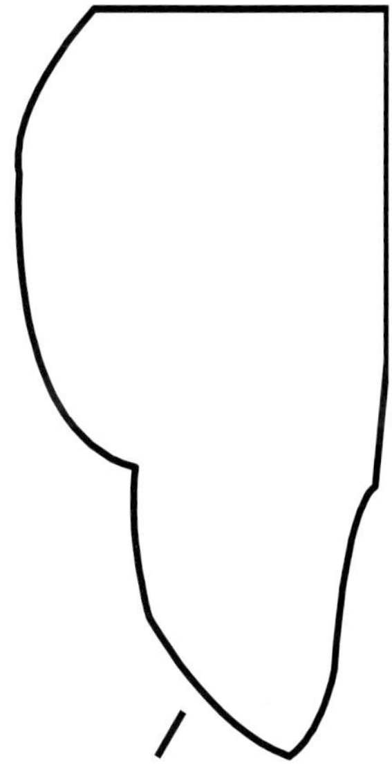

The intensity of friendship
isn't measured by how
frequently you meet.

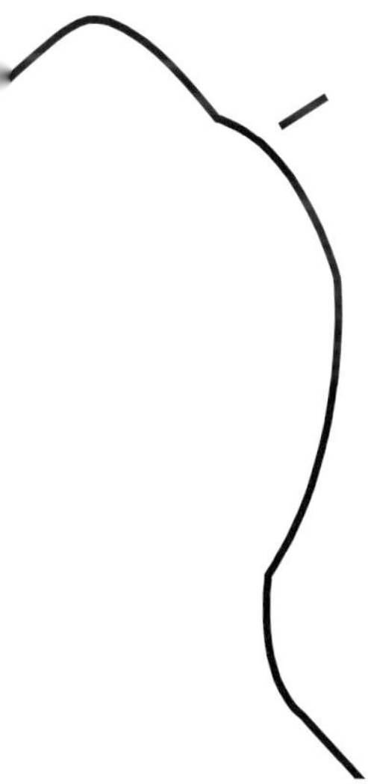

OCEAN OF FRIENDLINESS

No one knows what life has in store for us. We meet such people who bring about permanent changes to our lives, be it good or bad.

We're all sailing in our own boats on a vast ocean with our own load to move forward with.

During this journey, we meet all kinds of people, some with whom we grow so close and form an unbreakable bond - friendship.

Some experiences may not be as pleasant, as everyone is different. These are the waves that shake you up, but at the end a calm ocean awaits you.

It's upon you to change your perspective.
Everything will seem so much better.

"Every little bit of stress you eliminate contributes to a more productive day. That's not being a diva; it's placing yourself in a situation that allows you to be in optimal form."
~ Lilly Singh

Some things make us realize who our true friends are, and those who tag friend with their name for a false reason.

Many such opportunities come in our life,
It is upon us to know them and open up to see the difference.

What we always see may not be true, but feeling, experience and affection says it all.
It is on us to realize it on time.

It may hurt sometimes,
Someone you feel so close, may not actually be.

Who I felt was so close to me,
Turned to be so far,
With all the fights came sadness and heartbreaks.

I couldn't believe it!
I was never ready to believe it
But I was forced to

The dilemma was
Should I lose a close one?
Or see the truth and support it?

The truth it is,
As said, the truth is always bitter and hard to believe.
It does come up late, but the truth always prevails

The truth changes from bitter to sweet in a matter of time
And it seems to be the best thing ever!

Shedding tears does not always ease pain,
Sometimes we need that one person to talk to
#Friend

Even when you have a lot of people around you, you still feel lonely.

It is just like a crowd of people from whom you stand out.
When you are in your own world and thoughts, but visually, you are all together.

Such people are usually difficult to understand because they don't portray their presence of mind to all expect selected people whom they trust.

And gaining this trust takes long.

I have always heard,
That be it any relationship,
Friendship is always the strongest.

Probably it is because you choose your friends

Some who stay with you for life, others don't

It is not necessary to talk everyday, there's a special bond, an unbreakable bond.

Not everyone can understand that.
It goes beyond imagination and I have amazing friends.

Value relationships

Never stop talking or caring for each other.
Promote brotherhood from your side.
Always take the initiative to start.

Everyone will gradually learn from you
and take it forward probably

And when misunderstandings arise,
Take the step to talk and sort it out.
Otherwise grudges held can go on for
years and destroy generations to come.

I saw someone,
Probably talked to her for the first time
And it felt like, I've always known her,
Within sometime grew immense friendship,
An unbreakable bond,
And then came along a beautiful text,
Which gave rise to
"The Fantastic Two"
Making it a memorable day.

Looking back to that day, it feels amazing.

MAGICAL

Isn't it magical?
The way we make friends,
We knew no one,
And as we look back,
There is no hint as to what made us
friends.

I am so grateful for this magic.
The beautiful and powerful aura filling
my life.

...Under the sun,
Walking under someone's shadow
#Friend

Self-reflection

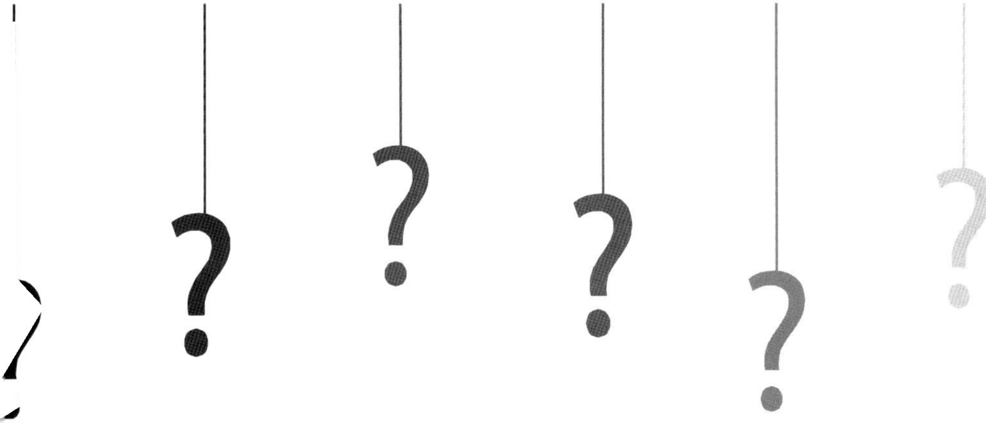

That annoying moment when you are confused and have no idea what is going on!

We have millions of questions and
things going on in our life each day,
that we don't give time to ourselves.
Never sit and ponder, nor relax.

It is very important to take that few
minutes of the day for yourself.
If you don't understand yourself, then
no one will.

ANGER MANAGEMENT

"I could reply with a middle-finger emoji, but that wouldn't be very productive."
~ Lilly Singh

We often tend to get annoyed and irritated
with what some people do.
But have we ever realized that we are the
ones who help them succeed in what they do.

The more we show that it affects us, the more
they will continue

We tend to make assumptions and opinions
about people and then whatever they do
annoys us, be it good or bad.

And then we answer back or say rude things.
Maybe not intentionally, but we still spoil our
character.
Then what difference is there between them
and us?

After going through so much, I am sure I
would not approve to be like one of them and
so we have to ignore. Not in a bad way of
course.
At least one has to act maturely and that will
really make you a better person

PATIENT?? YES/NO

Sometimes you like someone so much that whatever they do, you still give them a million chances to change.

But after all this patience, if there is no change, then think about it once again.
You really like that person, but do they like you back to see all your efforts of tolerance?

You should never do something with the intention of getting back, likewise, never expect affection, and care from people.

But after the million chances, you shatter! And at that point no one can bring back the time lost.

Though you cannot do anything about it, never change to be liked by someone who doesn't deserve you.
You are unique; don't lose your identity by trying to be someone else
The strongest and patient one is that who can forgive and forget after going through it all.

You always learn that you know you never want anyone to be hurt because of you, as you have experienced the painful journey.

ARE YOU LUCKY? YES, I AM

Everyone is lucky in different ways
It is not always clearly visible

But have you ever thought about it,
You being unique also makes you lucky.

And nothing is there solely by luck,
It is all a result of hard work combined
with destiny,
Then what has to be is always there.

As always said, so much to do, and so little time.

That is very true but we need to know what needs to be done first, and what comes next.

Prioritizing and organizing is very important in life otherwise you will never get anything done on time
Even though you have only one thing to do and all the time needed

TAKE THE FIRST GLANCE WITHIN YOURSELF

We always feel others are luckier than us or happier than us, and we wish we could be them.
But that is just one part of the story.

A lot of times to get there, people face a lot and all we see is one side of the picture.
Everyone has his or her story to tell and I am sure you do too.

You need to believe, trust, and respect yourself so that people do the same.

Always dream big.
The higher you try to go, the greater the risk of falling.
A hero is one who has the courage of taking that risk and rising again if life brings you down.

We often keep complaining about
things that go on in our daily lives,
And we also move on and learn to
accept it with time.

Then comes a time when we are looking
back to that day that changed our life,
and if not for that change, everything
would've been different.

Learn to embrace change; it has a lot
of surprises waiting for you at the road
ahead.

It may be long and bumpy, dark and
lonely,
But at the end, it's all worth it

Sometimes a dream leads to a great achievement, sometimes a talent, or sometimes a hobby.

Always be yourself and stay alert. You never know what way exactly will bring you a great opportunity and achievement.

Catch hold of every opportunity. If you don't succeed, at least you made an effort and trying again is always an option.

BE YOURSELF

Don't live life copying others.
Create your own identity so that people
know you for who you are.

Of course you will have a role model,
Use that person to guide you, not make
you live like them.

Be bold and be strong to try new
things,
You may be the new trendsetter.

EVERYTHING IS WITHIN YOU

A problem seems big or small based on how you see it.

An achievement seems enormous based on how many people we share it with.

All pain vanishes seeing a smile on a loved one.

These are the small hearty gestures that make living an art.

For the love of writing

You may be bound by speech, but your
message can still reach the audience by
pen

This legacy has been going on since
years,
Where pens were not in existence,
carvings were used

Your words can impact someone's life,
even one person
This is how to initiate change, silently
and gradually.

In the end, it does work.
Some people may feel motivated and
understand your words and some people
may feel provoked and try to prove you
wrong.

In both cases, you have done your part
because these words turn into actions.

I've learnt from somewhere,
That every story reflects its writer

That is because a writer usually lays down feelings and emotions onto paper and some further take it to action on the big screen.

Everyone dreams, visualizes, and thinks and of course everyone does this differently

Writing, becoming an author is an art appreciated by only a few. A writer has an advantage because the world can see the thoughts and visions through words

The wise one will analyze and see what you clearly meant.

Words kill like one thousand spears

The way you phrase each and every sentence makes an impact on the reader.
The same message can be put in positive or negative content, and this reflects the writer's mindset and thought process.

Don't totally give yourself away to your readers,
Keep some kind of mysterious background and anonymity.
They will always come back for more

Remember words can never be taken back once shot!

Writing so much sometimes also makes
me ponder from where the words came.

I see it as my imagination and thoughts
speaking.
A stream of words flowing, the more it
is stopped, the faster it flows and
catches full force.

You have the freedom of speech!
Don't bind yourself by fear,
There are a lot of ways you can send a
message.
The use of literal and harsh words is
not at all required.

Feelings can be expressed in a lot of ways.
Writing it self has various forms such as poetry, haikus, texts, paragraphs, stories and notices.

Writers have a hidden meaning in their words.
Every word written is an expression, sometimes openly, sometimes not.

Reading rather than browsing can see the actual meaning.

Occasions

Everywhere blooms the spirit of
Valentines Day
All red and pink, hearts, teddies, and
chocolates everywhere

This is a lover's day
Some people do not believe in it or feel
lonely because they are single

It is not only for couples but also for
anyone you love, your family, and
friends.

The day is just an excuse for
celebration and what is better than
that?

Have fun and share happiness around.
Surprise someone special, and his or
her smile becomes the best return gift

Spread smiles, spread joy
This Valentines Day!

A woman plays many roles, be it of a wife, mother, daughter, sister, and she symbolizes so many colors of your life.

White – she struggles to bring peace
into everyone's life
Orange – Although slightly, but has
anger in her towards correcting her
loved ones
Maroon - immense love and care since it
is a darker shade of red
Almond – neutral and multi skilled
Neon – brightens up everyone's life
around her

All these colors make up woman

Women are priceless, beyond
estimation

HAPPY WOMEN'S DAY

MY ROLE MODEL, MY LIFE

There is a woman,
The most beautiful woman,
My role model, my life

I always see love in her eyes,
I always see compassion in her gesture,
And a smile on her lips,
My role model, my life

From her I learnt patience,
And from her I learnt discipline
My role model, my life

She is my mother

HAPPY MOTHER'S DAY

SHE HAS...

She has within her the entire universe
The glow of her face like the morning
sun

The fairness of her skin like the moon
Every breath like a cool wind
Her touches as soft and smooth as silk
And her immense love which is
unbeatable
Being with her completes everything

My mother is one in a gazillion

HAPPY MOTHERS DAY

```
I N S P I R E           S
N   T       D           U
N   R       U           P
O   O       C O U R A G E
V   N       A           R
A   G       T
T           E M P O W E R
E                   O
                    N
                    D
                    E
                    R
```

THE WOMAN OF TODAY

Professions

PROFESSION...WORK...JOB...ROLE

In our society people are mostly recognized by the role that they play.
Be it of a student or of a manager, we are always playing our part

However, are all professions really appreciated?
Lets take an example of a police.
It takes a lot of hard work both mentally and through physical training.
They are here to protect us but every time we see them, most of people get scared and misjudge them as bribe takers.

Try talking to them politely instead of shouting at them; all they are doing is their duty.
And if one person isn't good, that doesn't mean that everyone is the same.

It is very important to appreciate the roles that everyone plays because even if one of them wouldn't be there, our life would be very different, maybe not even as safe as it is today.

I looked around and saw everyone so
busy,
Some sat in air-conditioned offices
while others having their backs
towards the scorching sun.

What I saw in common were their
expressions
Some smiles and some frowns, some
worried and some relaxed.

You're all equally important to this
planet.
To see how life would be without them,
try doing everything yourself.
It will probably be worse than living in
Stone Age too.

Appreciating all job roles on May Day
and everyday.

Inspiring through hidden messages

...UNDER LOCK AND KEY

Will my secret stay safe?
Who can I trust? - A lifelong friend? -
Or my diary?

If my secret is out, I will become the
talk of the day
I may lose a dear one

But what about those who die as a
martyr everyday?
Their voice is lost just as they depart
from this world

Their story is kept a secret...under lock
and key

We need to realize what to keep secret
and what not

Spread the story of the oppressed.

DREAMING? ALWAYS

Dreams pave the path for your
destination.
Something you want to reach.
Sometimes people will laugh at you and
taunt you.

Not because you are not capable, but
because they are unable to see what
you can see.
You need to have the power to convince
in order to get the required support.

And to everyone else, trust the power
of dreams. They may come up with
something entirely new that words can
describe.

Who is considered to be good?
The one who answers back to an adult or the one that listens quietly?

Majority will answer "the one who listens quietly"
But we should also look at literally, opposing an adult in something they are wrong or correcting them doesn't make you a bad person.
It depends on the way you do it!

There are various ways to put forward facts without hurting others.
It is necessary to stand up for yourself.
You need to know the rights that you have towards yourself and respect them.

No one can use you unless you allow him or her yourself. Sometimes you have to say "NO" and that can be very difficult.

WHY?

The tag we always move around with.
Do we ever think twice before asking
'WHY?'

The quality of a wise person is not by
the number of questions asked,
Rather it is by the content – then be it
one.

PATIENCE IS A VIRTUE.

I have always heard this saying, but a moment made me realize what it really means.

Some things are bound to happen in life, and each thing that happens has its own significance, meaning, and importance.

We just have to wait for the right time as God has always planned the best for us.

She walked down the street, listening to the chatter of talking, the tapping of shoes, the laughter of kids, the chirping of birds, and the hustle of trees.
How often do we experience this?

We have 24 hours in a day, but are we really using that properly?
We must allocate time towards our self be it to meditate or ponder.
Being at peace of mind makes everything better and produces positive vibes.

People spend a lot to get better work done.
You don't only need to be qualified but also need the presence of mind.
If a problem occupies your mind, then even the best person won't be able to do something that he has always been doing.
Think about yourself as well.

WHAT IS LAZINESS ACTUALLY?

Is it really fair going around and telling people that they are lazy?
There is always a reason behind an action.

A lazy person in actual sense is one who has all the resources available, and knows what has to be done, but still doesn't do it.

Before taunting anyone, at least make sure you know the reason behind what is happening.

This will lighten up humanity and make the world a better and happier place.

The world I live in is too colorful.
A lot of things are hidden from my vision.
Looking for the true picture has now become a struggle, because beneath all the colors still exists shades of black and white.
That is the picture of truth, humanity, brotherhood, and trust.

She had a house, a huge house, a luxurious house, but she was in search of a home.

She had everything that someone could ask for, but there were no people to share it with.

Then there was that girl staying down the street, she had a small house, basic needs and good food.
She would pass by this house everyday, and this is where she found a home.
Where people living with love and caring for each other.

It is the people in a house that make it a home.
Share, care, love changes everything.
Then a home becomes a place that people look forward to go to, after a long day.

...AND WHAT ABOUT TOMORROW?

I live for today, but what about tomorrow?
I leave all my worries to enjoy the moment, but what about tomorrow?
Today is my best day, and what about tomorrow?

Leading a trouble free life is a good approach but we cannot ignore the future. If we don't work hard today, then our tomorrow won't be as good as today.

Life is a real struggle, and we learn a new thing everyday.
Absorb every new thing because it is the experience and knowledge that will help build a brighter tomorrow.

When you are told off, you are hurt

When you fight with a close one, you
are hurt

When you feel the world has turned
down on you, you are hurt

Through all this, a best friend walks
beside you.
But when that friend turns you down,
then nothing matters anymore because
everything shatters.

At least give others the freedom to
express their feelings and emotions,
then none of this would have actually
happened.

I was standing at my window, looking down at the street. A lot of things were going on simultaneously, the daily honk of the cars, pedestrians walking by.

One thing caught my eye amidst all of this.
On the mid-crossing of the road bloomed one flower, it was beautiful, stood tall and glistened under the morning sun.

I couldn't take my eyes off that flower.
After a while, a butterfly sat on it.
I cannot say for how long I gazed at it.

I spent my weekend learning a valuable lesson.
Even if you are alone, stand firm.
Maybe all may not notice you, but those meant to, will find you in a matter of time.

I wonder why this generation doesn't think for themselves.

We were left with a legacy, a culture to retain and move forward with.
But at some point, we are leaving that behind as if it is a load.

Celebrating, and spreading happiness is good, but why do we celebrate something so pointless?
I see "Happy April Fools Day".

In the first place, what is so happy about it?
And what kind of joy is there in fooling someone?

You may not know but this may hurt someone, and some things that hurt take long to heal, or never heal.

A friendly joke is fine and does not have to wait for a particular day.

#SpreadSmiles #SpreadHappiness

Some days feel so pointless and lazy because we don't do anything other than sleeping or just sitting around.

Sometimes watch TV or read a book. But have we ever realized how that activity alters our imagination and thinking.

The next day we have a different perspective.
Sometimes, lazy days are beneficial; they help you relax after a long week and enable to boost thinking and the speed of working.

There is an awkward silence in the
room.
I am not alone but I cannot speak a
word.
The people with me were not strangers,
but the silence still persisted.
Although I knew them, I had nothing to
say.
I had a blank expression on my face.
I wondered, who would break this
silence?

Why do our words get misinterpreted
all the time?

And then we are told off for something
we didn't even mean to say

So whose fault is it?

And if we try to defend, it is
considered as answering back, which is
not entirely true

Never jump to conclusions because you
cannot read people's mind.
It is wise to understand rather than
forming assumptions.

Some people are considered mentors
for a reason
But what about when they violate it?
Then the apprentice also has rights and
can decide for him or herself with
complete freedom.

Learn how to fight for your dreams and aspirations.
If you have the capability of excellently describing what you want, anyone can move forward with your dreams leaving you as a vague image.

No one will ever ask you about the
hardships on the way,
They will only look at the end
achievement.

That is why the bee is always praised
and the mosquito swatted.

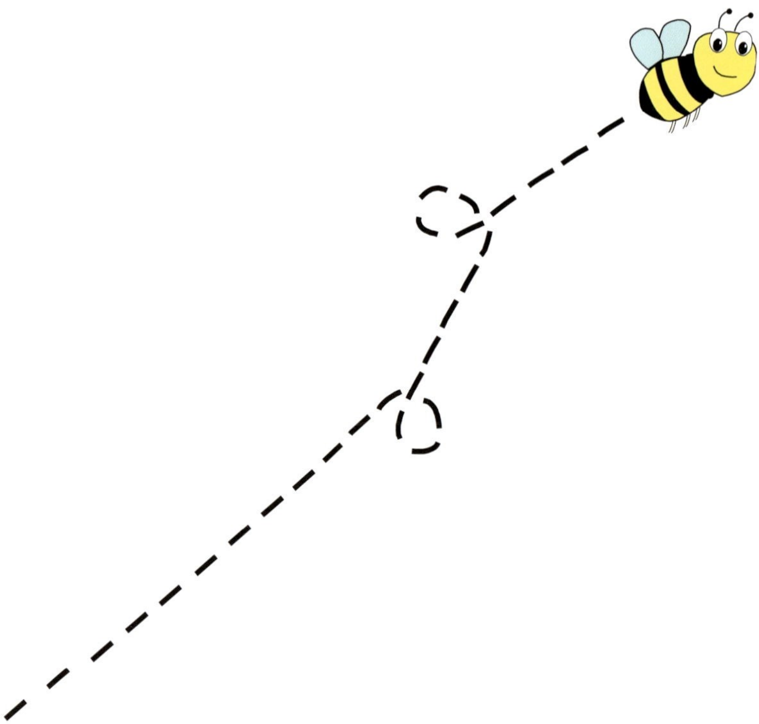

When you have something to say, SAY
IT!
When you have something to write,
WRITE IT!
When you have something to do, DO
IT!

If you don't do it at that moment, and
forget what you really wanted to say,
write or do;
The feeling haunts you the entire day.
Making you feel incomplete and
uncomfortable.

I looked for help,
But I felt alone.

I tried asking my way about,
But it was a foreign land.

I looked around,
All I saw were new faces.

I couldn't understand where I was,
Why was I there?

But after I fell into a deep pit,
I awoke from this nightmare.

Any problem that comes your way comes with a solution. The only difference is that the problem is visible but the solution is hidden.

Go where your heart takes you, it may show you the solution that is not visible to the eyes.

Fun to read...Abstract pieces

It's difficult to say,
I am a word used everyday

Day in, day out,
Year after year
My meaning becomes vague
It's difficult to say
I am a word used everyday

I reconcile between people,
I also break relationships,
I am far away from ego,
It's difficult to say,
I am a word used everyday.

Everything is amazing,
Everyone is so nice
Just before you can see the reality

It is so sad,
How everything changes
Within a blink of an eye

That you don't really know,
Whom to trust
And what is nice

Beauty lies in the heart
Beauty lies in the words
Beauty lies in modesty
Beauty lies within

It is not the dress that you wear,
It is just the feeling that it gives you
Beauty lies within

Each person is beautiful
In a different way
Beauty lies in talent
Beauty lies in art

Beauty lies everywhere,
Just look from the eyes of your heart.

Life, experience, and growing are great teachers.
When we are younger, our parents protect us from everything and as we grow, we see the world outside our comfort zone.

Always struggling for many reasons.
We actually see who cares for us.
It teaches us a lot of lessons then, whom to trust and on what basis to trust.

We should never run away from situations, rather face them, and become strong because now being independent is important.

I saw the rain pour down above my
head.
The water drops trickling down my
face.
The scent of wet sand spreading
around.
I felt fresh and reenergized.

I was alone; the street was deserted,
the sun hidden away.
It felt like everything I had done was
flashing in front of me.
I stood there by myself, seeing some
moments I had remembered, and had a
vague memory of others.

It was time to ponder, to remember,
and go back to what I had done and
what I had to do.

Did I have a purpose in life?
Or was I moving on with the flow?

What have I achieved in all these years?

An interesting conversation between diamond and coal.

C: Diamond, you are the luckiest stone
D: and why is that coal?
C: you are so pretty and everyone admires you, but no one even notices me, and if they do, I am thrown around, however you are handled so delicately.
D: but I feel that you are luckier than me. I alter people's emotions, some being happy, and others jealous or envious.
I have a constant risk of being stolen and you are always safe.
I am locked away most of the year, and taken out rarely.

Put yourself in place of the diamond or the coal. Both have their benefits

and drawbacks.
So who is luckier?
There was a huge garden in front of me, and in it were billions of flowers, each one of each person.

I was told to pick one that had my qualities or my thoughts, and I wondered, how hard can it be?

I started my journey and moved on excitedly for a few days, then that excitement died down.
Then came exhaustion and frustration but I did not get that flower.

I kept searching for it and as I saw other flowers, I wished they would be mine, not knowing what was in store for me.

I finally reached a waterfall and thought it was the end, but then from behind came an angel and walked me through that waterfall.

There was a beautiful pond, its water glittering with the sunlight, and there I saw my flower stand tall.

It was kept safely for me and only chosen people could look at it.

PUZZLED!

I have been playing a puzzle,
I fix a few pieces everyday,
The first pieces I fixed now have
blurred images on it.
The bigger my puzzle gets, the more
distant it looks.

This is life.
We don't remember everything we do,
But we have a few clear memories and
some vague memories of our earlier
years.

I am violet - I am neutral
I am indigo - I bring along peace
I am blue - I show the significance of water
I am green - I am down to earth, yet high above
I am yellow - I spread brightness
I am orange - I show anger
I am red - I show love

I show a lot of emotions and elements that are important in life.

I AM A RAINBOW

"Don't give up before you even try."
~ Lilly Singh

Everyone deserves a second chance,
then why not me?

I am just another human being,
Seeking perfection does not always
make me perfect.
No matter how hard I try, I still do
have faults within me.

Then why am I made to feel sorry all
the time?
Even when I make no mistake, why do I
feel guilty?

Not being able to do something is fine
as long as you have tried.
The biggest failure is in giving up
before the first step.

...AND I WAITED.

I sat on the staircase, looking at the rain
pound on the concrete before me,
And I waited through it.

The sun came forward, moving away the
clouds; I saw puddles that the rain left,
And I waited through it.

All I wanted was to take a perfect picture,
But I lost a lot of moments because I
waited.

No moment will become perfect by waiting,
Every moment captured becomes a memory

If I would have captured the rain, or the
kids playing by the puddle,
I would have gotten my perfect picture

Now I will not wait any longer,
I see a beautiful rainbow,

I will capture that in my camera as a
memory forever.
At the beginning of a journey that seems
endless, how do you feel?

Then we start that journey with a lot of
energy, goals, and discipline.
How do you feel?

And as time flies, we are half way through.
How do you feel?

Soon the entire journey ends, and all we
are left with are memories and moments
to look back at.

But this journey doesn't end here.
It goes a step further increasing the
hurdles every time you cross the earlier
ones.

Every student can relate the most to it.
Always remember one thing, learn to live
the moment,
Sometimes, that is all you have left.

Parents teach us everything when we are young - How to talk and how to walk.

They make decisions for us when we are still learning about right and wrong.

At a point they trust us and let us take our own decisions.
They're always there with us guiding us throughout, and when they correct us, we must understand.
They are the ones who will sacrifice everything but get the best for us.

Showing trust and respect is a great way to show gratitude towards them, even though we can never do for them what they have always done for us.

The beginning of every new journey
brings a lot of unexpected things.

Some good and some bad, we overcome
it all and reach the end.
Sometimes, we don't, and we fail
through the journey.

There is no giving up.
Rise as many times as you fall and
emerge as a winner.

Every journey has a unique way of
testing you; it brings out your hidden
talent that you never knew existed.

Every journey molds you and teaches
you life long lessons, and amidst all this
change,
Never forget humanity and kindness.

A MILLION SHADES OF BLACK

The colors that began were black and white.
In the context that people speak, they are not considered colors.

Black is the only color that stands out with everything and symbolizes a lot of emotions.

Stars shine brightest in the pitch-black sky and fireflies are visible at the darkest hour of the night.

Black is also associated to horror and also to glamour and grand.

It is your perspective that changes definitions and boundaries.

What is your shade of black?

The real world and imaginative world
are two opposites.
Imaginations can merely exist.

You need to balance yourself so that
you can imagine changing the world and
staying put in the real world to know
what to change.

You include me in all your actions,
I am apart of you.

You don't realize my existence,
I am a part of you.

People love to see me with you in a few forms,
If I change too often, I get everyone worried,
I am a part of you.

I make all your pictures worth a fortune,
I am a part of you.

I am present in every action that you do,
No one can separate us,
I am a part of you.

I am your emotion, whether happy or sad,
I will always be with you.

SMILE AWAY...

Start every week afresh,
Forget all the grudges and bad moments.
This will surely make you have a better year than last.

#PositiveThinking #PositiveVibes

Take a moment every morning when you open your eyes to think about what your goal is,
And what you are supposed to do to achieve it.

Jumping straight in to the day won't help us end it any faster, rather make the 24 hours seem to last forever. Ultimately causing frustration, anger, and destruction.

Wake up and calmly think about what is to be done and do it at the right time! And always have in mind I can do it!

#PositiveThinking #PositiveVibes

You are always with me
Haunting my day

And at night
I cannot dream because of you
You're my biggest nightmare

I prefer staying at home
Because I never want to meet you

You're the meaning of fear,
The cause of terror

Let kids be happy again,
Let girls be safe again,
Let men be alive.

Stop hatred.
Looking at the human side of you will
make a big difference.

Evil is only the absence of good.
There is no evil by itself.

The current wars and killing show an absence of peace and prosperity that once secured the earth.

Therefore, you cannot put your actions as a result of the society.
If you lack good within yourself,
You automatically give rise to evil actions.

I have been searching for a path since years.
I always reach a cross-section and take quite a while to decide which path to take further.

Trusting my instincts and parents guidance has brought me a long way with a lot of good things in my life.

Once again, I have reached a cross-section, quite confusing and complicated.

This time, the words that I have been writing have shown me the way.
Shedding bright light on the path I should select.

I would love to see what lies ahead.

I am a gesture of love,
or a symbol of blood.

I am soft and smooth,
or prickly and cruel.

It is upon you on how to use me

True love won't prick at all
Anything false and I will reveal it

Although I can't speak,
I express emotion in depth.

I am a rose

Empowering the mind

I write a lot of motivational texts and
some may think that it is not practical
to actually implement it.
I totally agree...

It is not at all easy to keep calm at a
difficult situation and think positively.
It is possible if you can tune and
control your mind.
Don't let your **mind** control you

This quality comes from a lot of
practice, sacrifice, and strength.
Thinking logically, crying at a problem
will not solve it but make you weaker
and tired.

Before judging people, it is necessary to know the entire situation that they have been through and what they are currently going through.

I don't think people have a lot of time to actually sit and do all that unless they have no work at all to do.
So it is upon you if you want to portray yourself as jobless and idle.

I hope and feel that this can reduce the rate of backbiting and putting people down.

Let us make the world a happier place to live.

Some people try very hard to break your confidence, pull you away from your success and goals.

Don't let them win. It is only a mind game that will last for sometime.

At the end, they have wasted all their time and energy putting you down that they remain at the same place as they were, while you progress and grow.

Don't complain when you come across such people.
Their action is just a result of insecurity and considering you above themselves.

To end with, I hope this has helped you find your definition of happiness, and this can always change, so try reading the book with a whole new mindset the next time you pick it ☺

You are free to use any of the quotes or texts for personal use, however, please reference the author due to copyright.

I would like to end by saying that each person in this world has his or her happy place. Once you have found yours, do make an active effort to help others who may find it a little challenging. Maybe a slight push from a happy person can lead them towards their own wonderful definition of happiness.

Thank you,

Mehreen XOXO